BETWEEN WARS
AND OTHER POEMS

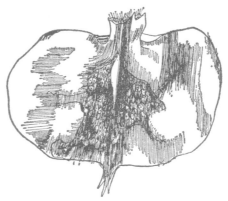

BY ANNE HALLEY

*THE UNIVERSITY OF
MASSACHUSETTS PRESS*
1965

For Jules and Mary

CONTENTS

BETWEEN WARS

YOU CAN EAT YOUR CAKE AND HAVE IT ONLY IF YOU EAT TO VOMIT

About restitution, say this,
the money is nice. Buys schöne Aussicht, Schlagrahm,
Rosenthal and Rucksack (my bitter, modest Wermut)
O lovely handy twenty
years later. Neither mangled, crippled
nor marks, no bruises on it. Honest cash money
healthy as when last seen, separated,
kissed goodbye–
(Besides, I was hardly born, no more than Horst Eichmann;
it was my father's business)
Why where have you been my darling
and how long I thought you
one with dentures, gold teeth, babies' bones, the glue pots
of the world had had you–
(And why should they get fat on it? They're getting more than enough)

Let's know ourselves my treasure.
Come Bundesbahn together.

> Ashes Ashes
> fall down, all, fall down

Can you know how it was? There were little dripping fountains,
the inn with icy linen sheets, so heavy,
and a fogged dawn when the Easter fires
swam milky up the mountain.
Trips across a small country, tree-lined roads,
narrow and twisting, through plow-rippled hillsides,
then another landscape, purple-flecked, flat.
There are great boulders piled to mark
an ancient burial. Here you lost the kite, a sulphurous
storm was coming up. Did you miss the stork,
tall in his nest? He is red-legged in the cross-piece gable
of a thatch roof. He brings luck.
This is a village, the main street cobbled,
the geese honk, swarming.

> Buttercups and daisies,
> and the ditch has a thick scum,
> stagnant, green, growing.

Do you know sun-slippery paths in woods with porcupines
end in an overflow of yellow wheat?
You can crack seeds between your teeth,
pick garlands, sing, dance in a circle.

> Red poppies, blue cornflowers, gold sheaves of wheat,
> I have a white dress,
> we give thanks for the harvest.

No. Fat tourist in your postcard mind.
Garland, lucky stork, and Easter fire
are gathered and garnered; one lightheaded travel morning
you stood in a rose arena, dew-silvered brick, not quite finished,
steps stretched far into treetops.
Jungbrunnen. What was it for? In your sleep
the giant circle
filled with gathering Jungvolk, tangled thickness,
raised arms and banners and muscled swell: burst mouths.

> Nevertheless, this mill on this water
> across this field, also that walled garden.
> That parched woman with the twitch in her cheek.

Your name on these stones.

My two grandfathers
had yellowing white chinbristles, and sat
in highbacked green plush scratchy chairs, next to
tables covered with long fringed cloths,
vases, framed oval photographs (cut velvet), straw flowers,
peacock feathers, clocks gilt-trimmed in statues, next to
pianos dressed in paisley, bearing more vases, photographs
of finetooth-combed greataunts tightly buttoned, Biedermeier fans,
and Blackforest nutcrackers.

My two grandfathers smoked
Meerschaum pipes in separate rooms, not for ladies,
and descended
not at all to the soapsmooth stone of basement kitchens
where laundry often boiled. Black coal scuttles
stood in every room, no–not in bedrooms. There
eiderdowns swelled pregnant and gaped
from white casings.

My two grandfathers
were always served first at table and could
slurp soup if they wanted (the soup would be lentils).
The plates were deep, scalloped, the napkins
rolled up neat and tight in rings, and the knives
lay on thin silver knife-rests between courses.

Also my grandfathers had through the years
numerous children in long aprons, and they
tyrannized their daughters. I could not help feeling them
very much alike: both spoke high-German,
thought first of education, and
were loyal to their Kaiser. Only
one wore a skull-cap, read Torah, and lost
his only son to a marriage; the other was a hunter,
beerdrinker, kept a gun, and lost
his son to a boxshaped, windy airplane.

They lived in the same town and of course never greeted each other,
and each died lucky, in his own bed, much later.
At least, I was told so.

Always prepared for revelation,
when Grandfather brought the pheasants home for Christmas,
I sat behind the tree and wouldn't talk;
they should find me reading a big book,
whispering poetry.
There were angels continually in my mind, then,
or a bareback rider,
something with spangles, wings, four or five white horses,
and long hair floating out to catch a star.

I liked the Christmas tree, self-reflective, baubles
you see yourself in, all surrounded by lit candles
that make a real halo, liked princes, crowns, roses,
liked having my hair curled,
waiting to be chosen.
And many of my kind and country
were chosen at dead of night, heard the big boots
crash upstairs, terror in tinkling glass, while
I wore a crown of flowers on my seventh birthday,
curtseyed, made penwipers, learned to write in ink,
every Christmas recited a long poem,
ate raisin cake on Sundays
in sunny rooms full of Sunday flowers and clean air.
How can I say the terror
grew there? That one day the marvelous bower
behind the tree and the winter garden
among the near-dragons, moons, fabulous, spiralling over the
          doorway,
said to me, yes, there is a secret for you:
be afraid.

High up from some severe
Evangelical Reformed Heaven
a lady I never saw frowns disapproval
on starchless descendants, ragged family duty,
spoiled religion, lapsed housekeeping, and the frayed-out ties
of Godly knit authority.
The lady is a determined
non-determinist. For her all was choosing
Right. All her life friends had to be cut dead for their
wrong choices, frailty, selfwilledness; with all the
linen sunned, rugs beaten, vegetables put to soak,
the catechisms and the categorical hard crusts,
in the end she talked to no one;
but set her husband's food out neatly
on the scrubbed white board of the kitchen table—
a round bread, sharp knife, blue bowls of cheese and meat
covered with a clean cloth—and departed.
From an upstairs window
she watched her fleshly grandchildren hold hands
and cross the street; always packed, she travelled
from one intolerable human habitation to another
finding further
impossible disrespect and laxity.
She sent letters back unopened.

Tante Ulla, Tante DiDi, Tante Tienchen,
Oh wie trau-er-ig, Oh friends of my mother,
girlfriends, old friends, Oh my godmothers
of whipped-cream Torte, doll clothes, masquerades and boat trips,
of summery garden house picnics,
all for children with good manners
and all unmarried. Oh untold hordes of German
female second cousins, friends' friends, pensioners, teachers,
and many of you widowed.

Tante DiDi, Tante Tienchen, Tante Ulla,
whose brothers and lovers tossed their schoolcaps
so gallantly, turned them in for helmets,
cheer the volunteers of '09, the class of 1910. Oh their nephews
and great-nephews froze as cruelly
in broken boots before Russia in the forties.
All ladies so proud, so mannerly, conventional,
pouring out coffee, lifting sugar in tongs
at the goldflooded breakfast window,
embroidering in hoops, and quarreling
with the slovenly, uniform-mad Mädchen
who would oversleep, be disrespectful.

You too, Tanten, starved and skulked in cellars,
foraged for potatoes in back gardens,

more than once took walks to the country
to scrounge a half of sausage. I know you grew thin in a passion
of march-time music, suffered, burned out for a nation,
did you also say, Sieg Heil, in your hearts,
Basta, Prosit, to the windborne stench
you might not dare to know? Tante Tienchen
we visited for plum cake,
an old old lady on a cane, martial up the mountain,
and she said, Oh how they have humbled us.
It cannot be borne.
Struck her cane on the ground in 1950, 1930.
We must not give in.

I see a stucco villa under trees,
the housecat on the windowsill asleep,
(it could have been) a hallway tidy, deep,
the wicker table's doily holds a bowl
half-filled with cards, pins, bits of fluff; the stairs
are plain, with squeaky matting; in the Saal
soup vapors last, but certainly one sweeps
out faithfully, and tablecloths are white
though they must do the week and therefore hang
most accurate at corners, darned with care.
(Was it like that?) A usable Pension
like others, homely, neat; the weekly bill
in thinly rusted ink on the lined sheet
at breakfast with your roll? your room perhaps
too small? a brass bed, washstand with
the pitcher's surface intricately crazed
filling the modest looking glass? I see your face
complex and secretive, insomniac;
you powder lines old in mistrust—a skin
crosstracked, like worn cloth, dry—and in you mourn
missed recapitulations, promise, pieties unkept,
causation; 1866 to 1940. Dead.

The same old plod of sluggish blood,
and self-indulgences, and dreams of gulls.
A small, echt deutsch disease on cobblestone
and sidewalk brick with moss
between the stones, and must be near a harbor
that's full of hootings for the interned heart
to brood and feed on. Tonio's complaint
I'll call it. Incubation, long. Prognosis that
these symptoms are their remedy. I disapprove

         Yet love
blazed through the schoolyard in a goosy crowd
of half-grown girls, all nervous arms entwined:
the brown rust gate to shriek
as if unhinged; a blurred-by bobtail head;
a rubber coat to flap
the rained, chalkmumble school-befogged November days;
a gay windstiffened billowed back to sail,
my eyes caught at the hem: I see
its crossweb texture and the pebble soles
of scuffling kicked-up boots.

And that the virus took.

On any street
preferring wind off harbor and a sea
I'll question ankle, shoulder, back of head,
for one so seen, against all sense, the fled
stubborn unfinished, hoped for, incarnate.

Germans in the Sunday park. Ein Volk. Family
whose speech I try to hear. All commonplaces.
They're blond enough, like me. Plain people we would have called
    them
at home, between wars, when gracious in possession
we could grow learned, good,
lucky, could buy
some knowledge cheap: sniff the sour baby
and turnip steam, the curtained beds in hallways,
stale air from housework rags, moisture from swamps
under Elfriede's apron, and the arms
rattling our pails and coal. She ate fast and wore drab.
Meanwhile, I learn in school, don't look at all
at naked heads, sheared of their lice and pride.

Now see this child, how fair,
how ear-ringed, ribboned, braided,
and flower-sprigged, how wholly foreign,
Ein Reich, herself, she struts, strikes poses
on stilted legs in common roadside grass;
weaves daisies for her garland, hums, and speaks
a lovely singsong lilting
half-language of her own.
Now peace and fashion
ride on Frau Mutter's bulk; she's tailored
ample and smart, with rollicking crimped hair, with powder
prospering cheeks. And her bleached man, jobholder,
no different now from other fathers. Yet I think
his clothes fit tighter, or his sleeves

are rolled too tense and high. Or memory
dissolves him backwards, fixed, flat as a poster
threatening the cellar door: Kommunist, Nazi,
streetfighter, hungry malcontent, rockheaver,
and that same face: nursemaid's blond bogey beast, halfbrother,
who makes me most myself
fearful: Alive.

Such phantoms can possess me, fret, obsess,
me with all otherness, all misheard sound, blank eyes,
that still might strike me dumb. Arresting, flutter
the irreparable heart. Old violences
we skirt in this encounter, old remorses,
the racing heats of blood
I lust for still: that bones might rise to shatter
through history
us to a common word.

I

Between wars a world was made. Take inventory:
dead uncle's sword on the wall, one flashy helmet,
gold eagle screwed on top. The old gentlemen swear
by cavalry, by Kaiser. Friedrich
der Grosse was one hero. I loved an empress
and the young Fritz who gave up flute and friends
for glory, glory, glory.
They say Barbarossa waits under the mountain,
and Siegfried, Jung-Siegfried bathed
in dragon's blood. Herrgott, may all our enemies
the sword cut down.

Between wars the boy makes campaigns
in the Christmas rooms: three green papier-
mâché mounds, hollowed, with revolving cannons,
one Big Bertha, files of grey soldiers, two flamethrowers,
four dead Frenchmen—staggering, wildly flung,
two stretcher bearers with hands pierced for carrying,
one polished fieldkitchen and one fieldmarshall,
von Hindenburg in lead, taller than the rest.
There are also barbed wire
in proper tangles, and connecting trenches.

Towards 1920 in the Berlin winter the babies
were wrapped in newsprint. For years die Arbeitslosen
marched. Later Krista,
prettiest in our grade, took me aside.
She said, Ask your mother for old clothes. In the Volksschule
I learned to jeer at Catholics,
was taught stories: childhood of our Führer—
imprisoned, like Luther, he wrote a noble book.

And biblical history. Now irony
is the easiest confusion,
but thirty little girls once lay in wait for one
to be surprised, beaten. Self-righteous,
class honor betrayed, we talked it up: we hit her
with our bookbags and shoved her down the stairs.
Then, ashamed, we let her go.

What is on my conscience is a cry I heard
one of those years—Hilfe, Hilfe—from a closed house.
We walked by with the grown-ups who may not have heard it
or know better than to interfere
in what is no one's business. I am glad I heard it, although
I have not had that chance again. A human voice
crying for help is odd, infrequent
even between wars.
And of course we couldn't help it.

2

The world is made and children grow between
wars, recognize themselves, the world, and war;
we are ourselves, the world; and children run
with tightening fists, with pounding piston legs
to search out war and beat the earth for love;
we are the world each day's new rage unmakes
when the flawed heart in anguish shakes the floor
and tongues of fire burst the well-wrought roof,
eyes burn, glass shatters, breath comes hard
minute by minute between wars: the world
is made. We have the evidence. And wars
remake us, and we them. Herrgott, I live

Each day I must relearn
my ABC of crime
some committed by me
some for me, in my time

Accused must answer
where were you when
whose place was taken
days you were born?

Born from pits, on graves
we make our beds and lie
guiltily with our loves
afraid, afraid to die

Criminal murdered
maimed mowed-down dead
make room, move over
pass and be buried

Each day I must relearn
my ABC of crime
Accused Born Criminal
live in my time.

The Unitarian minister
was pinkjowled, worldly, not austere.
I held my flowers hard. They shook,
and our respective parents took
the tragic view. They were as pale
as we were green. No one could tell
if this would work, or if it ought.
I can't remember that I thought
of you, jobs, money, babies, if
this too were something to forgive—

At any rate, it was not bliss.
Too much forewarned, our wedding was
as grim as any truce. I blame
myself still, and my ingrown shame,
my gaggle of Germanic genes,
and my intemperate fear of change.

My father etymologized
the name by which he was not pleased.
Your father could not eat our food.
Baptized and circumcised, we stood,
the queasy creedless who appeased
no one but Emersonian god.

The signs and portents were not good,
though all drank wine. For weeks I could
not keep my breakfast down; I choked
and, gagging, wept. At last we looked
on our done deed and separate son,
straight as a weed, eye-dazzling, strong.

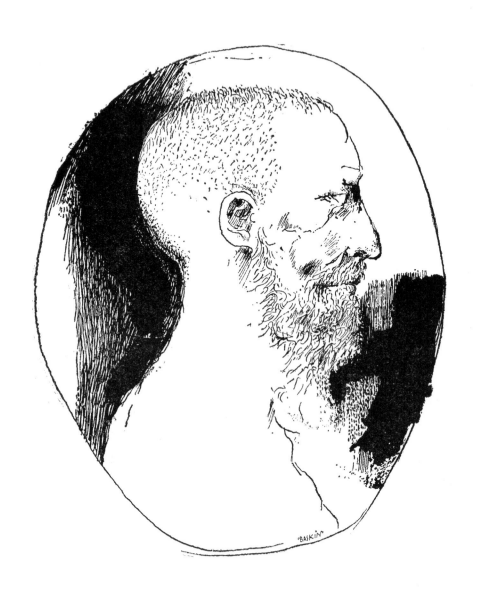

OTHER POEMS

Dear God, the day is grey. My house
is not in order. Lord, the dust
sifts through my rooms and with my fear,
I sweep mortality, outwear
my brooms, but not this leaning floor
which lasts and groans. I, walking here,
still loathe the labors I would love
and hate the self I cannot move.

And God, I know the unshined boards,
the flaking ceiling, various stains
that mottle these distempered goods,
the greasy cloths, the jagged tins,
the dog that paws the garbage cans.
I know what laborings, love, and pains,
my blood would will, yet will not give:
the knot of hair that clogs the drains
clots in my throat. My dyings thrive.

The refuse, Lord, that I put out
burns in vast pits incessantly.
All piecemeal deaths, trash, undevout
and sullen sacrifice, to thee.

COMEDIES OF LOVE

1

How praise, appraise, the comedies of love
and not die laughing? Years, I moved
thick and spasmodic in my growing pain,
skinned knees and elbows, clown's feet, stumbled in
such corkscrew brooding, black jawgrinding nights
and ecstasies of doubt, mute promises–
Not, now, where have these gone? No loss.
But who could stand it? Laughing, must
and love I will. Not die of it, not sink
into my self's old shame, not break
on pride's clown tears and hiccoughs: Laughing shall,
hysteric, cauterized, love love's survival.

2

Elusive as burnt feather taste of dream
dreamed curtained, swathed, quiltbogged. A mingled sweat
in other people's night, the bedroom set
too much like someone's house, or someone's death
of houses, weighty, secondhand, awry–stale thought
stored in a snored-through house, a smell
something like memory, queer, shut-in, yet caught
steaming off pillows, under closed doors curled
too faint to catch. A keyhole smell, thick air
in memory hung, foreboding. Breath like fear,
noxious, alive. A spring creaks to come true.
Knowledge and dreams. Hands smell of you.

3

That children's bodies move me more than yours.
A shallow line, milk-breathing, tender fur,
the naked shoulder and the collar bone
flushing in sun–the carved, the miniature,
that will not last. That will not stay for me.

Radical pleasure, tempting hands to own
dolls' visionary flesh. Perversity
humbling to name: what, in the name of love,
would grow most sweet where most, it cannot have?

4

What partings, and in tears. You'd think
to part had been our purpose—but to cling,
to strain against rough cloth, to break apart
a finger's breadth, to turn to touch again—
to swear no use, no good can come, and burn
for more, for all no good: so might our best
our clearest, dearest loving purposes
cry out at parting. What persists, denies
not tears, not force of love, not mutual use—
blunt terror, sliding off from the masked eyes
of pain-besotted lovers, willing loss.

5

This bed, our world, that is
a jangling iron, edged
like any battle car,
closed tight by plates of dark,
goes clanging into walls,
makes plaster crack and fall—
O brave upon that hulk
declaring total war
on butcher, banker, all
reasoning daylight men,
we'll loosen legs and sleep,
honorable warrior.

And what has carried us to this,
that we should lie, slick-skinned as fish,
naked as born and as infirm,
vulnerable as the unfurred worm,

That we should thus ourselves reduce,
confound day's dignity and use,
leave walking upright and regress
to wanton in our weaknesses?

Dear love, our weakness with our strength
is measured in a finger's length.
Brought low to ground, we put down man
to make him rise where men began.

A private, gathering passion filled
the belly where our child was willed.
Slow-ripened, where we were most rash
his present jolts us in the flesh.

This curl of life and rudiment,
this scratch in time, was passion spent.
Our double self-forgetting lies
behind the child's unfocussed eyes.

The birthpang and the twitch of love
we took to bed, forgetful of
ourselves and him: prodigious act
how strangely one, in child and fact.

Spread-eagled, in a lover's leap
our son has hurled himself to sleep.
His few day's muscular selfwill
roaring, let go, and dropped him, still.

So fast, so deep, in such great noise,
rests, sleeping, all that sleep destroys.
The deaths we ripen rock his bed,
shutter my fallen son's blind head.

It is a backward and last summer wind
rattles and warms the gutterful of leaves,
threadbare, skeletal, twittering at my feet.
Wind to confuse the cleanswept autumn mind
with green wings flashing in the eye's despite.

It has been summer here, and fall. My season had
its roseate mornings, furled and damp as buds
to cast a steaming shimmer on the air;
there have been nights like lakes, round lakes that lay
far inland, sweet and sluggish; there was heat
curling green shoots to ashes. Now the leaves
are brittle singers, flitting ghosts of birds.

Though wind can tease me into images,
ideal tears, and easy summering,
the bald autumnal sky holds up a light
hardened with frost and, as the window cooled
my forehead when in dreams I used to count
desire's footfall, lumbering through the dark,
this chills me now: the moment is its time.
The small boned bird, the leaf, lived and have been.
And frail protectives, eye, transparent pane,
cloud with my breath, or love, or time between.

Mirrors distort nothing. They hang all
asymmetries, bulbous offenses, bases
that make a self on the preposterous wall.
Hang all my always unknowing faces
unfairly finite, to infinite spaces.
Repeat, resurrect, exist, to mock
selves met anew the same, past change of places:
The glasshouse cannot need a lock.

There was a curly mirror in the hall
and it was framed by gilded knobs and laces
of cupidbows and flowerettes. My doll
looked just like me. Two stolid kewpie graces
we stared alike. Our mirror image chases
my realized singularity, the rag arms block
my goings down new halls, choke with embraces:
The glasshouse cannot need a lock.

This mirror knows what dull face to recall.
Out of the toychest limbo litter races
a shadowdoll whose sawdust siftings fall
around my dullard feet. The doll step traces
what progress, steps, what doll-like paces
I–measured in the mirror–dully took
and overtakes: we merge in our old stasis:
The glasshouse cannot need a lock.

Mirrors make clear analyses
and outline facts in disaffected shock.
Mere-mirroring, they state their cases:
A glasshouse cannot need a lock.

Go barefoot home, on crooked toe
hot heel on scorched pale stubble,
strained tendon, swollen ankle slow,
stumble, foot-sore, on rubble,
  and go, and go, go barefoot home

Go barefoot home, go claim the calf,
pig-tender taste grows tender.
With tattered toe, on crooked staff
leans home the lout offender,
  and go, and go, go barefoot home

And sing the song with cracking lip,
tongue stumbling, parched, and sore.
A burnt child steps too slow to slip,
else I'd be falling more.
  and go, and go, go barefoot home.

What years have been away? this crazy land
is green again and wet. The grass will grow.
And I am ambushed on the riverbank,
must grope to fit some feeling to a spring
and put an edge on blurred remembering.

I have been so asleep, love, that I dreamed
a frozen winter, hollow in my heart.
Last night the rain was warm when I looked up
through fat burst branches in fantastic bloom
and now the crazy grass—Love, I must know
what news of you has let the winter go.

They wore light dresses and their arms were bare,
paddling backwater seasons, moonstruck, coy,
who cooled their necks with pale green spicy scents
and spread skirts stiff in petals as they sat
dazzled, waiting becalmed; and one might lift
hair bright as buglings on the wind.
All princesses.

And someone came, or would come soon enough
whose common words were stranger than the spell;
whose quick and faintly furry hand might not
fit those curved palms; would have been glad to stay
stretched flat, count polished pebbles, wait, and sun
a young brown back, pretending to be earth.

And not a prince. His breath was dark and sour.
He was not tall. But he was chosen. Chose,
and so must come, perhaps in the new moon.
Awkward himself, and shy, would learn to be
Mariner, Swineherd, King,
and set one free.

There is a pride for young men. The hero,
eyes shy, demanding, deep with mother tears,
the pale young god whose bones crack bare
whose edge is all put on
with shattered arcs:

Glad gut of childhood,
sweet prison, closed room, arms, and her fat bed
shed, unshelled, out from soaked voluptuous laps
from cradling sheet that fed his curl of sleep,
and pared from rounder cheeks
now wholly knife
unsheathed is ruthless
with the double edge, regret.

Purer than innocence, translucent frailty
of unstilled flesh–O motherless–
who plucks it out, the milkwhite sucking tooth,
shall sharply hang
shall most be set on edge.

My hero is a dry fire and angry
so much tinder, burning for self, who trembles
and bites his tongue on love.

Dear friend, dear Scrooge, dear critic, dear my friend
    and gentle heart and man: though seasons send
    no bells, no star, no angel dripping love
    through slushdim jangled streets, though from above
    grotesque, the screaming jets will shake our tree,
    frail-branched, already brittle, still let's be
    content to approximate mythology.

Though we achieve no miracle, but live
    the common discontent, vexatious, stiff,
    and stuffed with minor ills, and get no grace
    and doubt the time and often curse the place,
    in short, are human, let it be enough:
    let's joy in unredeemed and graceless love,
    let's honor birth, like ours, among the beasts,
    and celebrate all partial lives with feasts.

They were together a long time. Five or six months,
years even, with interruptions, and shared a bed
often enough, knew each other's
linty pockets, verse fragments, damp attic closets,
and family letters, swollen with exhortation.
They were seen hand in hand at snowbound street-crossings,
Doppelgänger, unkempt in government surplus parkas,
or sleep-frowzy, mopping up saucers in the cafeteria:
friends, siblings, rivals together, but surely
too daily for lovers, too grubby for passion,
too much the same,
slumped down, chain smokers, far back at public lectures.
Who saw them last? Did they
grow up at last to the formal division of union,
he to a briefcase, she to her children?
What can have become of them,
living a life, here, plotting on yellow second-sheets,
and sharing a cart at the automatic laundry?
Where did they go? They loved each other.
It may have been more than convenience.
One kind of marriage. A long time together.

FIRST MOLES OR MICE

First moles or mice,
limp sucking animals, snouty,
all pointed to clamped jaws,
they hang at breast, their
best resting place, or roll, curl up
round on the warm lax muscle pouch
they may remember. Face down seems
their natural position: root, dig,
slither, scratch; they move forward first
in gurgled spasm. How their eyes,
opened, seem watching inward, register light
but turn back, count
liquid, internal rhythm.

      Those bobbing foolish heads

You have to touch them.
Feel the heat, the aureola,

      around the unset skull.

The baby at my breast
suckles me to rest.
Who lately rode my blood
finds me further flood,
pulls me to his dim
unimagined dream.

Amulet and charm
against dark's harm,
coiled in my side,
shelter me from fright
and the edged knife,
despair, distress
and all self-sickness.

One sister has the brightest curls,
another has a lissome walk.
A sleep-logged father soughs and turns.
A mother hardens in the dark.

And one must cry before she sleeps
and nightsweats curl the other's head,
while father's goatheart skips and leaps
and mother's bones lie flat in bed.

In rush of blood and tides of chance
my sisters stutter in my throat.
If father snores, who'll watch me dance?
My mother's hands have veins like rope.

Annexed behind the Lakeview Inn
the aged mothers wait for mail,
cook dinner in their separate pots,
hang nightgowns out to dry, and smile

At me across the fraying lawn
and backporch mop, with slops in hand
gesture and nod; ambassadors
whose speech I will not understand.

Old women's legs and teeth go bad.
The children grown, their old men dead,
they sun their brittle heads and shade
their eyes with folded Hebrew news.

My thirty years of pride and gloom
I cherish; doubting, would refuse
when in my low close summer room
the flesh sings simply, not by choice.

The simple old bring offerings
of applesauce, bring chocolates wrapped
in bits of paper handkerchiefs.
I am not grateful, but accept.

GRANDMA ALL-FORGOT

I'll say a prayer for sticks and stones,
for bitter gall and breaking bones,
for hairy warts and birdsnest heads,
for beaky slatterns, twisted shreds
of shawls and mildewed bundlings wrapped
around the skin-bag derelict,
the mumbling Grandma all-forgot
who haunts the hallway's cabbage rot.

Remembering tremors, evil-eyes, and twitches,
Pray God for shivering city Grandma hallway witches.

INSTEAD OF ELEGY

. . . those shoes were old.

I

And still last month I thought
we all had quickening bellies, heavy breasts;
it seemed the plains must steam
with procreation, milk, and muddled piss
and that full flood so hot
upon the languorous, lagging heels of such
portentous, reasoned courtships
I must think that yes
was all I'd need to know;
why then, I've lived
like anybody else as if we were
forever, and I had not thought
to practice much for this
that whores about all countries:

Well, here you are old bitch.
Come in death.

2

I have the new lamp
to light the dark corner. We have raised
the portrait exactly one-half inch.
Bought the cakes, left uncut
the hard good bread. There is a bottle of charged water
that no one else will want.
Madame, I saved a long time
to accommodate just the demands you might make.
A long time for just your hand
itchy to interfere, empty; light prickling touch;
O meddling old woman coming to your predictable

(lovely lady, I am still only beginning
to forget to hear you)
end.

3

Leavetaking once, I wept, half slept
listless past miles. Since, I have kept
through watery dreams, some fear of stones,
distrusted trees, foundered on towns.
We pass the towns that own their sky,
the cows fat with eternity,
and churchroofs fastened down by God,
tightly enspired. Loosed, my flood
unheld and judgmentless passed by
merely in tears. The houses stood
stony, the block affirms the square,
fixes the roadbed. Highways wear
us out of compass—a passing look
beds us to passage. Ground and will rock.

Through city is hardest. The street
will wind and whisper in wait,
will billow, curtained in noises,
possessive, window-boxed, with voices
that hold me nothing. Slept and gone,
leavetaking, I have wept for stone.

Unleaving might afford a life
careless, to walk in, or to drive
a car along—but transients wake
naked on roads. Left then to take
leavings only, who stays is passed.

We pass in failings, unmoored, misplaced,
misspent in tears. Go sleep the road:
leftover, driftwood, doomed to flood
and drowned in dreaming, whirled up and on
to some last inlet, some final stone.

4

I ask your pardon.
Probably you were neither
as good nor as bad as dying makes you,
nor should you be my excuse
for words. We were not related.
If, in the town where you died
I drank pale wine in a green lake of sun,
if the fishy boy
suddenly embraced me, that the boat rocked,
we were sick later,
doesn't matter naturally now,
not where we were
or you either.

Listen love, though we will prove
harsh, illiberal, cold, in love,
love dismembered will we need
deny, dismiss, and deprecate?

If our hands should lose this art,
pleasing in our pleasure's start,
and the blood, receding, prove
harsh, illiberal, cold, to love,

When the bone grown cold and stiff
shivering, rather breaks than give,
love dismembered, will we need
deny, dismiss, and deprecate?

Though we relearn lust in hate
and will maim to separate,
listen, love, although we prove
harsh, illiberal, cold, in love,

Fortunes lost, love, will we praise
once these have seen better days,
or, impoverished, will we need
deny, dismiss, and deprecate?

Harsh, illiberal, though we prove
disremembering Croesus love,
may we not in separate sleep
marvel how our leavings keep?

Rather may in separate sleep
we marvel how our leavings keep.

THREE FROM RILKE

UNKNOWN FAMILY

So they took shape: as dust solidifies,
perceived as one might glance into a corner
some empty morning: sudden grey begun
nowhere and to inexplicable ends,

of matter undefined; so they appeared
at the last moment in your path, and were
something unknown, uncertain, standing there
in the wet downpour of the narrow street

to ask for you. Perhaps. Or not for you.
Because a voice like one left from last year
sang out at you, and yet cried out in sorrow;
a hand you might have borrowed reached out to
your hand, then did not take it. Can these four
find one they mean? Who is it that must follow?

ONE RECOVERING FROM SICKNESS

As sound of singing comes and goes through streets,
first closer, and then shyly far,
wing-rustling, sometimes almost in your grasp,
then once more scattered wide on air,

so life plays games with one recovering
from sickness, while she—weak and yet renewed—
would give herself, is awkward, slowly trying
a single gesture, stiffened with disuse:

To love caressingly the hardened chin,
to lift so high the calloused hand in which
fevers have raged their contradiction,
and feel it like a blossoming of touch—
She apprehends it almost as seduction.

Because Lord, our big cities are the damned
are flight in front of flames, dispersal, loss,
because there is no help to give them solace,
and their small time runs fast—

And people live in them. Live badly, hard
inside deep rooms, are frightened, more tormented
than a young herd just brought in, still ungentled,
while your earth wakes outside, and draws its breath
but they remember nothing, and exist.

Children grow up there under windowsills
in an unchanging darkness where no sound
comes to them from outdoors, no flowers call
them to a full day's space, and joy, and wind—
but must be children, and are sadly child.

And virgins blossom, tentative and shy,
remembering childhood peace. But the unknown
experience for which they bloom and burn
is emptiness. These tremble and withdraw.

And live in closely curtained, draped back-bedrooms
their days of motherhood denied,
through long nights full of weak-willed vain complaining,
and cold years without struggle, without strength.
Far back, the deathbed waits in shadow
and draggingly they yearn to reach death's place,
and die a long time, as if chained to dying,
and are like beggars in their going forth.

People live there, white-flowering, pale,
who die of the hard world, amazed—
and imperceptibly through unmarked nights

a delicately smiling face
is frozen in a hollow grimace.

These walk about, dishonored in the service
of senseless things, by labor without courage,
their clothing withers,
their smooth hands age soon.

The pushing crowd will give no thought to spare them,
although their walk is weak and hesitant,
but homeless, beaten dogs will follow
a while behind them, shyly silent.

They are delivered up to their tormentors,
are cursed by every passing hour's bell;
they draw in, circling hospitals and clinics,
and fearfully await admission day.

Death lives there. Although not the one whose breath
they felt as children in prophetic touch,
but as one knows him there, a meager death.
Their own death hangs in them—unripe
green bitterness: a stunted fruit.

O Lord, give every man his proper death . . .

Well and yes, there have been angels
runners, long swoopers, feet slender as birdclaws,
feathered, these hollowboned balancers, not for dirt rooting
their airy rudders, on wind's smile, sun elegant, billowing,
borne up in curls and frothed, buoyant on sleeves,
air's love and breath in them—low fluttering hoverers
caught on fused motion, strung:
Annunciation.

Yes they were. And well, and angels. Fearsome
the tidings, saying fear and fear not,
be not afraid O fearful,
struck terror, from every rock an echo,
fear not struck fearsome
from any rock, the heart.

O doctor dear my love, admit
there are enough. Why should we need
justifiable worldwide fear,
whether the sneaky drug deforming
quietly, from inside out, or
the drizzle, firestorming doom
out there, invisible, swarming—
no scabrous ooze, secretive sore
and not the loosehung head
of what I saw led down the road,
an emptiness, a waste in bulging skin.
But this. Enough has not enough.

Dear ministrant, dear doctor
exhume this blade of flesh with your bright steel.
Come succor me, believable monsters.

On the other side, no easy matter.
Think on the others, love, my doctor:
think the milked male, the humiliating
dash across a dawnwhite street,
the locked laboratory,
but the semen caught, deliverable,
hot from the press; think, lastex lady
inside whose whorly layers nothing takes.
Think those slitherings, bedpans, trickles,
salt tears to float fishes
smell on only—

Think so much hard, some human, work.

Enough and not enough makes less.
Monsters we suffer as we will,
Old Sawbones, sorcerer, we waste
in rubber skins, in little death:

O dear my doctor, love, be still
Hush, surgeon, little friend, come fast.

What madness that I come like Halloween
in heels worn crooked, trailing hairpins, gloves
with thinrubbed, dingy thumbs, a lipstick smear
and safety pin no secret, unrehearsed
householder, matron, clumsy semblance of
the propped and proper bit, tricked out for this,
respectfully, to see my friend gone mad.

Disguised, uneasy, in the doubtful stuff
I never thought I'd bolster up to suit
my dear friend, now gone mad. And so ascend
with clutch of fruit and the wrong cigarettes
(never prepared, though warned) to the locked ward,
the top floor, station sixty, double doored, to see
my maddening friend, who wears no more disguise.

This hospital displayed me to myself
in arrogance. My prideful burden high,
Prima Gravida, perfumed, toddling in
past senile cancers, cripples, kids, the poor

Card-carriers from door to door, out-patients out
of everything but that. The thick-voiced poor
humiliated mumblers, shy in front
of nursery maid technicians and the coy

Tip-toeing interns who will find them out
in coughs and lies. Well, I was shaved and plucked
still steaming clean, to fear no rubber glove,
hardened for vaselined outrages and the row
of frothy samples, labeled, body-warm.

It was pride
brought me to this before, with health to spare
to thrive on any stench of spreading legs,
cheap privacies revealed, so many pounds
laid out in cubicles. But mine exempt.

But mine exempt. Or so the mind insists.
I'd be no numbered meat, no weighed-out case,
nor bossy driven down her gravel road
by hulking rubes, with peasant's hue and cry:
the wet side's heave, a bloodshot frantic eye,
a spread of fearful nostril, and a swing,
comical udders wildly blundering–
the emblematic puzzled female climb
to her true state.

We choose and are exempt.
Or so I thought. Although the birth was slow
and (natural's the word) to learn those ropes
was more than you could plan, and less once done.
You grip the handles, but the birth grips you
alone. Locked, shaken, then the bursting through
with all past choice unmade for this last one.
Or so flesh would insist. A day or two
blots out the unexpected climax, stitches heal,
you come back neat, closed, almost virginal.

Yet bodies made us like. My gossip, friend,
the tumbling breast, the heaped-up jelly thigh,
rank female flesh to swell in spite of bounds
and punishment: I watched you, dulled, with sweat-
ed quinine, ergot, baths, give up the lost
and bloody liverish lump; and watched you truss,
massage with cunning motors, starve, then stuff,
a body learned in value, shamed by use;
and see you at the dresser buckling clothes
cruelly tight; or breathless, fevered, wild
among jammed zippers, ripping seams, smeared pots
of salves and lotions, matted woolens, scarves
and dirty stockings, trampled like the fears
you'd measure round your waist, pluck out with hairs,

or hide with heavy red on the bit mouth
that gibbered love. I think we called it love.
And yet I never thought you mad above
some necessary excess, willed, endured,
for both our sakes. And might not love you cured.

They lock the door behind me. I am cold.
We are at sea. And soon this ship will small
and fully loosed, deny my guilty sight.
I feel a cable's ache and brutal creak.
What teased us parallel, will tantalize
no longer: know the inward shiver and the tic
expectant, with this shift from foot to foot
and distance in the dimming eye, milk-white,
a foggy growth like suspect cataract.
And am too chilled to kiss you.
O turn back.

But you ride high, unchanged,
still brave and full
of passionate discord, and tumble truth
and childish lies together. Crafty, strong
for bedpost gossip, exploration, pills,
you roister on your holiday of ills,
the long-awaited journey coming true.
New lovers and mad mothers pad the hall,
bright-haloed in your need, their need of you.
And I have brought this fruit.
Be rational.

You show three paintings I refuse to praise.
I go home angry and unrecognized.

a

A simple answer. As, an end to love.
Room emptied, cupboard bare, nothing to think,
drained mindlessness, heart's seepage, run-out loss,
a basin, rustringed, in a scoured dry sink.
I mean a boneless hand, mean broken glass
crashed in a dented pail, leftover words
thick on the tongue, flat yellowing of touch
dead to itself, mean ether's cage, silence
pressed to the ear, lips moving to no face,
a skinshaped crust, cracked bandage, a mistake,
a withering, and something scarred and shed and failed,
an absence answered, understood, an end.

b

Be hungry then. If that's a sign of life
let's welcome it. Now cold must settle in,
no mothering sun draws us, no sweetening
this flesh and blood awhile. Fat summer's gone.
I thought us safe, stored up fullbelly sun
smoothlayered, live, eased in my summer skin
to feed on while nights stiffen and congeal
could need no count nor care, no husbanding.
So wrong again. Here's anger like a dog
red-eyed, griped with a stinking famine,
will drop us shrunken, shriveled on hard want,
accountable, harrowed, beginning.

We enter on our middle lives,
what friends I had, resigned, changed, gone.
I live a wife like other wives
and live as best I can.

And I will praise someone:

Praise stiffnecked virgins wavering
down wooded lanes alone,
with proud young men, shy following
tight tendoned virgins home.

Also the child who wooed for warmth,
the stick-man, lucid, lean,
the athlete lover, counting thrusts
who hammered out his pain,

Praise the mad couplers, shattering lives
wildly, and fierce in want,
their bodies scattered on the air
affirming all dissent.

We enter on our middle age
and I will praise, not name,
some friends I had, well loved and left,
and left me not the same.

Lovers and learners all,
and fumblers in our day,
my ordinary loves,
transfigured, gone away,

And decorous wives and husbands,
nurturers, saving much,
recalled and known by heart alone
who once were known by touch:

I praise all learned loving,
all ignorance dispelled,
and innocences moving
in partings through the world.

If I could, I'd write
how glad I live and cultivate:
to put tomatoes in and squash,
green salad on a yellow cloth,
how especially the white and blue
plates please me then. Also, I do
ironing mornings, make my list,
go squeeze fruit, open corn husks, watch
the butcher while he cuts our meat
and tote up prices in my head.
Evenings, I shake the cloth and fold
clean sheets away, count socks, and read
desultorily, and then to bed.

All this, could I, I'd write to you
and—doctored—parts are almost true.
But this is so: some days I've seen
my neighbor in her curlers, frown-
ing intently, sweeping hard
her porch, her sidewalk, her paved yard.
Her serious eye, following broom,
penetrates to my scratchpad room
and so—on my good days—I sweep
the front porch hard, and hope to keep
a neighbor image in my eye,
good aproned neighbor, whom I'd try
to emulate, to mimic, be—
translate some certainties to me.

That mothers' meeting, visit, when
Elisabeth first felt her son
leap into life: Mother of God
and Prophet's Mother, forward bowed,
embracing secrets, each in each,

they celebrate each other's fruit—
cylindrical and gravid, plain,
I puzzle over what they mean;
what do they speak of, in what tone,
how calmly stand. If mortal men
could touch them thus—O sacred, grim
they look to me: this year, I'm thin
have cut my washerwoman hair—
yet they persist, so solid, there,
content to carry, bear this weight
and be as vines, initiate.

I have been fruitful, lucky, blessed
more ways than I can count, at rest—
or ought to be—and even thrive
efficiently: yet come alive
odd moments in surprise that I
should still expect, impossibly,
and at the same time wholly hate
my old expectancy. I wait
long past my time, like the old Saint,
but unlike her, I'll make complaint.

For when I stand here on the step
and sigh and nod my housewife's head
and wipe my hands and click my tongue
at dust, or rain, or noise, or sun,
though motion's right, I feel it wrong.
I can remember all my dolls'
tea-sets and washboards, cribs on wheels,
and the whole mess, the miniatures
of pie-tins, babies, plastic meals—
a dustblown attic full of wrapped-
up child's play. How begin, unpack,

through splintery crates and newsprint feel
the living child and make it real.

It's real enough. Inside my house,
uncustomed, unceremonious,
I seem to wade among the shards
proliferating, wrecked discards,
a whole decline of Western Man
in microcosm: who'd begin
to sort it out, make do, decide
to deal with this, to let that ride—
make love, patch plaster, choose your work,
your car, your party, and your church,
keep conscience, throw out sense of sin,
free impulse, but in discipline—
a ruptured rug, a beaten chair
stare at me, stupid as despair.

And I am full of anger, need
not words made flesh, nor wordless act,
nor cycles inarticulate,
have never felt a moral thrill
at choosing good against my will
and no orgasm, man or God's,
delivers long from my black thoughts—
Housewifely Guardians, sweeping yet,
sweep out their graves and ours: O let
those flourish surely on, who know
the laws in which they bear and grow,
let multiply, secure from ill,
vessels wellformed for grace to fill.

Printed in
Monotype Caslon
on Strathmore Bouquet.
The drawings are by Leonard
Baskin. Some of the poems first appeared
in *Intersection*, *The Massachusetts Review*,
Mutiny, *The Noble Savage*, and *Perspective*.

the University of Massachusetts Press